Body Books
Skin, Teeth & Hair

Anna Sandeman
Illustrated by Ian Thompson

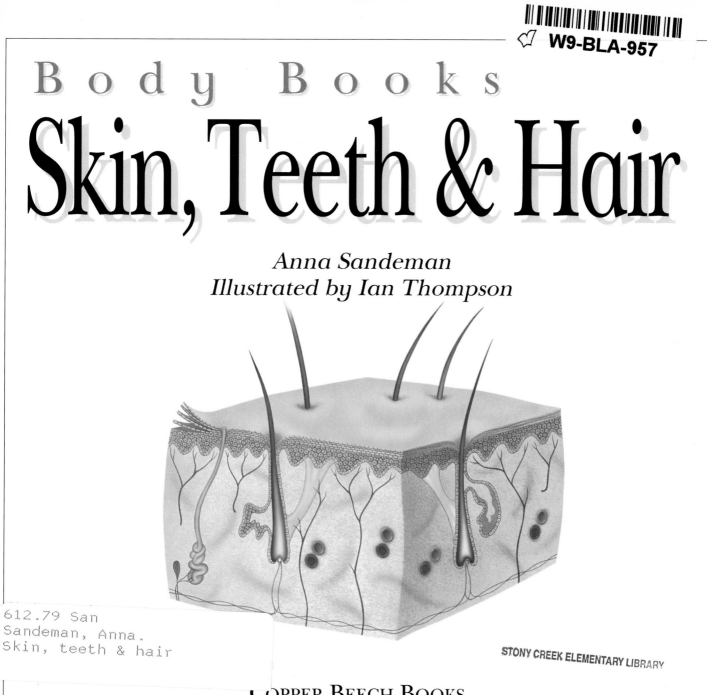

COPPER BEECH BOOKS
BROOKFIELD, CONNECTICUT

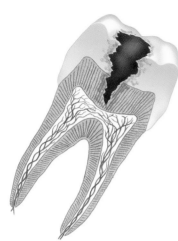

Copyright © 1996 Aladdin Books Ltd.
Produced by Aladdin Books Limited
28 Percy Street
London W1P 0LD

Designed by: David West Children's
Book Design
Designer: Edward Simkins
Editor: Liz White
Picture Research: Brooks Krikler Research
Consultants: Dr. R. Levene, M.D. and Jan
Bastoncino, Dip. Ed.

First published in the United States
in 1996 by Copper Beech Books,
an imprint of The Millbrook Press
2 Old New Milford Road
Brookfield, Connecticut 06804

Printed in Belgium

**Library of Congress
Cataloging-in-Publication Data**
Sandeman, Anna.
Skin, teeth, and hair / by Anna Sandeman; illustrated
by Ian Thompson.
p. cm. – (Body books.)
Includes index.
Summary: Describes the functions, characteristics,
disorders, and care of skin, teeth, and hair.
ISBN 0-7613-0489-4 (lib. bdg.)
1. Skin–Anatomy–Juvenile literature.
2. Hair–Anatomy–Juvenile literature.
3. Teeth–Anatomy–Juvenile literature [1.
Skin. 2. Teeth. 3. Hair.] I. Thompson, Ian,
1964-   ill. II. Title. III. Series: Sandeman, Anna.
Body books.
QM481.S26 1996
612.7'9–dc20   CIP AC   96-12646

Photocredits
Abbreviations: t-top, m-middle, b-bottom,
r-right, l-left
All the photos in this book are by Roger Vlitos
except: 6, 9t, 28bl &29tr Frank Spooner Pictures; 6-7,
7t & 28-29 Bruce Coleman Collection; 14-15 &
24t Science Photo Library; 29br Mary Evans
Picture Library.   5 4 3 2

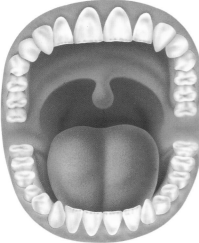

Contents

Skin types

All animals with backbones have skin. The skin may be thick or thin, rough or smooth. Many animals have a special type of skin which helps to protect them from their enemies or their surroundings.

A hedgehog defends itself with nearly 7,000 sharp spines. An armadillo keeps safe inside a suit of armor made of tough bony plates. An ostrich escapes scratches by having thick scales on its legs.

Other animals have skins which help them to hide. The chameleon changes its skin color to blend into its background. The leopard, which spends much of its day among the treetops, has a spotted coat which looks like dappled sunlight.

Human skin, too, helps to protect us against the outside world. Although we have no spines, plates, or scales, our skin acts as a barrier against injury and disease.

Your skin

Your skin is the largest single part of you. If it were laid out flat, it would cover a space of about 16 square feet (1.5 sq meters), the area of a twin bedsheet.

Most of your skin is about 0.08 inch (2 millimeters) thick. But on your eyelids, it is less than 0.04 inch (1 millimeter) thick. The skin on the palms of your hands and the soles of your feet is up to 0.2 inch (4.5 millimeters) thick. It is thicker here because it has to stand up to heavy use.

When you are young, your skin fits you snugly. Unlike a snake, which has to shed its skin from time to time, you have skin which grows with you. After the age of 25 or so, your skin becomes less elastic. Wrinkles and creases appear as you get older and your skin becomes looser.

The color of your skin stays more or less the same throughout your life. Its shade depends on how much melanin it has. Melanin is a type of coloring which protects skin from the sun's harmful rays. People from hotter countries usually have more melanin than those in cooler places, and so their skin is darker.

The epidermis

Everybody's skin is made up of two main layers – the epidermis on top, and the dermis below. As in all parts of the body, the skin is made up of tiny cells. New skin cells are formed at the bottom of the epidermis. They move upward until the older cells above are forced to the skin's surface. This takes about three weeks. During this time, the older cells die. They are squeezed and flattened together to form a tough outer layer which covers the whole body.

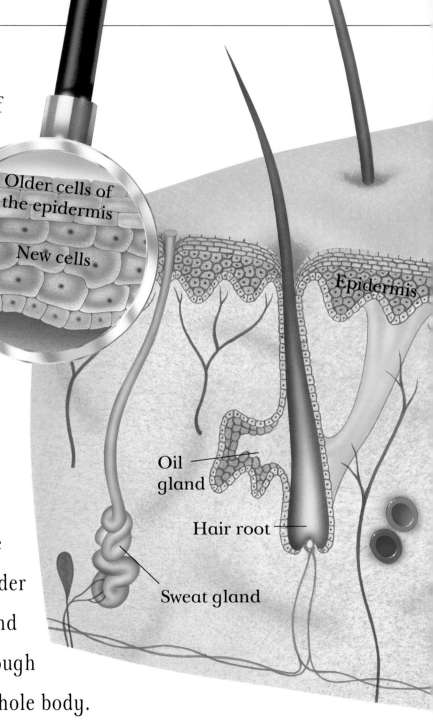

Older cells of the epidermis

New cells

Epidermis

Oil gland

Hair root

Sweat gland

Dead cells on the skin's surface

Nerve

Blood
vessels

Dermis

This outer layer is always changing. Dead surface cells are rubbed off your skin as you walk, sit, and even sleep. In just one minute, you may lose as many as 40,000 cells! But don't worry, your skin won't wear out. New skin cells are being made all the time. As the old ones fall off, the cells below are pushed up to replace them.

The dermis The dermis contains nerve endings, blood vessels, hair roots, and sweat glands

Your nerve endings can tell if something is hot or cold, rough or smooth. They can also feel if something is hurting you. So if you prick yourself, your nerve endings send a warning to your brain that your finger is being hurt. Your brain then tells your muscles to pull your finger away.

Your blood vessels, hairs, and sweat glands work together to make sure your body does not get too hot or too cold.

The green arrows show the direction of the nerve signals.

When you are hot

Blood vessels widen to carry warm blood closer to the skin's surface, so body heat can be lost. This is why your face gets red if you have been running hard.

Hairs lie flat against the skin to stop warm air from getting trapped.

Your sweat glands make more sweat to carry body heat out into the air. The hotter you are, the more sweat your glands produce.

When you are cold

Blood vessels narrow to keep as much body warmth as possible.

Tiny muscles pull on your hairs to make them stand up and trap warm air between them. You can see these muscles working when you get "goosebumps."

You do not sweat.

Defending the body

All around us there are millions of tiny germs. Your skin stops these germs from getting into your body. Cells on the skin's surface overlap like the shingles on a roof. They form a strong barrier which few germs can get through.

Your body is also protected by natural oils, which coat the surface of your skin. They are made by glands in the dermis, and contain chemicals which kill attacking germs.

Close-up of the gland which produces the skin's natural oils

14

This oily coating helps to keep your skin supple, and to stop water from seeping into your body.

Even so, skin is not entirely waterproof. If you sit in the bath for a long time, your fingertips become wrinkled and soft. This is because your skin is becoming waterlogged.

Close-up of the layers of cells on the skin's surface

Teeth

Most babies are born without teeth. The first teeth appear at about six months of age. By the age of about five, most children have a full set of 20 "milk" teeth. Shortly afterward children start to lose their "milk" teeth to make room for their adult teeth. These appear gradually over the next ten years or so.

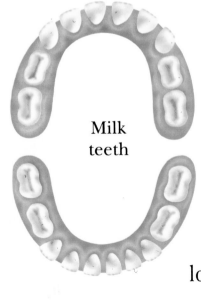

Milk teeth

How many teeth do you have? By the time you are a grown-up you should have 32, although some people never get the four back teeth known as wisdom teeth. Once an adult tooth is lost, it is gone for good.

Canine

Molar

Look into a mirror and open your mouth. Can you see that your teeth are different shapes? At the front are your incisors. These are sharp teeth used for cutting and chopping. The pointed teeth on each side are your canines. Their job is to stab and tear food into small lumps.

Behind them are your molars. These wide, flat-topped teeth chew and grind food until it is ready to be swallowed.

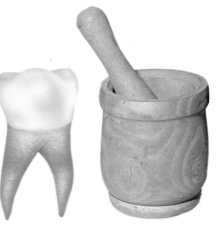

Inside a tooth

When you look into your mouth, you see only the top half of each tooth. This part is called the crown. It is covered in tough, white enamel. Enamel is the hardest material in your body.

Dentine

Pulp cavity containing blood vessels and nerve endings

Crown

Under the enamel is a layer of bonelike dentine. The dentine protects a soft horseshoe-shaped area called the pulp cavity. This contains the tooth's blood vessels and nerve endings. Signals about pain or extreme heat or cold are sent from here along the nerves to the brain.

The dentine and pulp cavity reach down into the root of the tooth. Front teeth have just one root, while some back teeth have two or three roots. The root is attached firmly into the jaw bone by a kind of bony glue called cement.

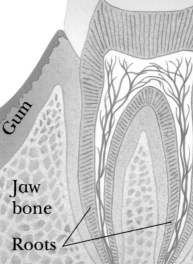

Gum

Jaw bone

Roots

Healthy teeth

Although your teeth are hard, they will rot if you don't take care of them.

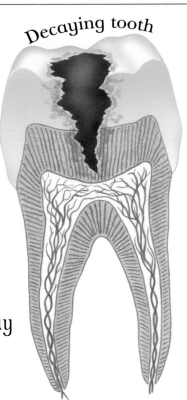

Decaying tooth

Food left on teeth attracts germs. Millions of these germs gather on the surface of teeth to form a thin layer called plaque. The plaque makes a kind of acid, which eats into tooth enamel. If the plaque is not brushed away, the teeth begin to decay. Once the decay reaches the pulp cavity, a toothache may set in.

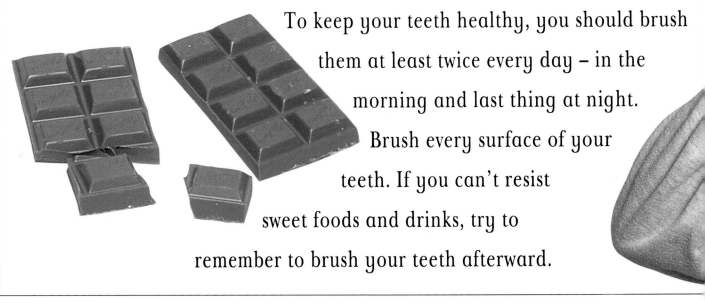

To keep your teeth healthy, you should brush them at least twice every day – in the morning and last thing at night. Brush every surface of your teeth. If you can't resist sweet foods and drinks, try to remember to brush your teeth afterward.

Eat more foods that contain calcium, such as cheese, yogurt, and milk. These will all help to keep your teeth strong and healthy.

Keep your teeth in good shape by eating crunchy foods, such as raw carrots and celery. Give your gums a treat by eating fruits with lots of vitamin C, such as oranges, tangerines, and strawberries.

Follow this simple advice and you should keep your teeth for life.

Hair

You have hair over almost all your body. You have two main types – the fine, soft hair which covers most of your body, and the thick, stiffer hair which covers your head and forms your eyebrows. Only the palms of your hands, the soles of your feet, and your lips are completely hairless.

You have more hair in some places than others. On your head, you have over 100,000 hairs. Each one grows about a half inch (1.25 centimeters) a month.

After a few years, a hair stops growing. It rests for about three months, then it starts to grow again.

If a hair is left uncut, it may grow up to 5 feet (1.5 meters) long. When a hair has finished growing completely, it falls out. A grown-up loses about 100 hairs a day.

Older people often find that fewer hairs grow to replace those which have fallen out. Their hair may get thin. Many men become bald.

How hair grows

Every hair grows from its root in the dermis layer of the skin. The root is inside a kind of tiny tube of skin, called a follicle.

Cells grow together at the bottom of each follicle to make a tough material called keratin. As keratin forms, the hair grows up from the root and out of the follicle. The cells die as they reach the skin's surface. Only the root of the hair is alive, the part you see is dead.

Even the hair on your head is dead. The reason it looks shiny and healthy is because each hair has its own oil gland at its root.

Close-up of a hair

24

The gland covers the hair with a light

coating of oil to keep it in good condition.

If the gland produces too little oil, hair will

appear dull and dry; too much oil and it

will look flat and greasy.

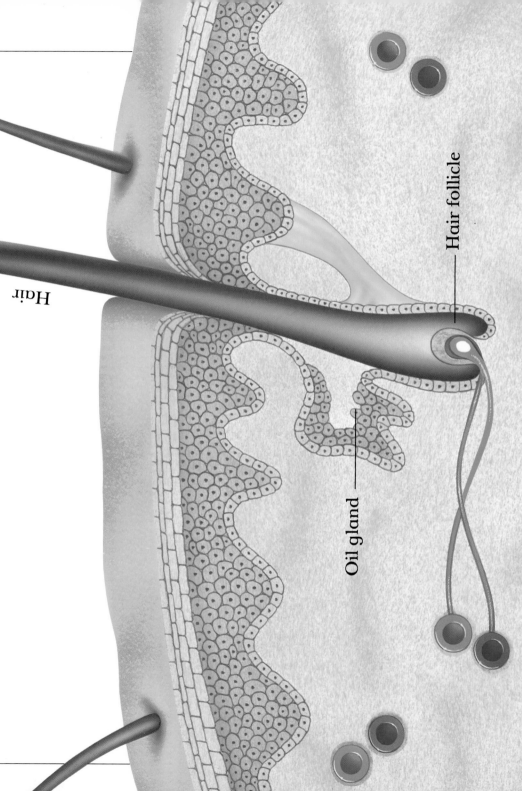

Hair

Hair follicle

Oil gland

Types of hair

The type of hair you have depends on the size and shape of your hair follicles. If you have large follicles, your hair will be thick and heavy; if you have narrow follicles, it will be fine and flyaway.

The shape of your follicles decides how straight or curly your hair will be. Straight hair grows from round follicles. Oval follicles force hairs to bend and become wavy. Flat follicles coil hairs into curls.

Round follicle

Oval follicle

Flat follicle

Your hair color is probably like that of your parents or grandparents. It may be black, brown, red, blond – or any shade between. Your skin color also affects the color of your hair.

Make a chart showing what color of hair each of your friends has. Which is the most common color of hair?

Hair	Number of people						
Black				4			
Red		2					
Blond			3				
Brown						6	

Did you know?

... that your fingerprints took shape while you were still growing in your mommy's tummy? They are different from everyone else's in the world.

... that sharks grow row after row of new teeth, which move to the front of their mouths as their old teeth wear out?

... that a rhino's skin is 12 times thicker than yours?

... that false teeth were first worn by the Etruscans over 2,600 years ago?

... that fingernails and toenails, like hair, are made of keratin? The longest nail ever grown belonged to Shridhar Chillal, whose thumbnail measured 52 inches.

... that about 200 years ago some men and women wore fantastically tall wigs? Mice were sometimes found nesting in them.

Glossary

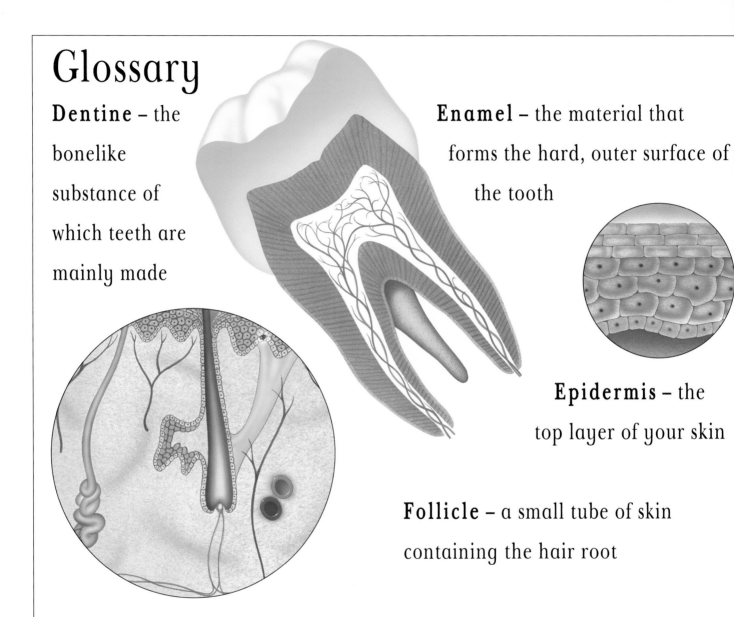

Dentine – the bonelike substance of which teeth are mainly made

Enamel – the material that forms the hard, outer surface of the tooth

Epidermis – the top layer of your skin

Follicle – a small tube of skin containing the hair root

Dermis – the bottom layer of your skin, containing nerve endings, hair roots, blood vessels, and sweat glands

Gland – any part of your body that makes a substance that can be used by the body

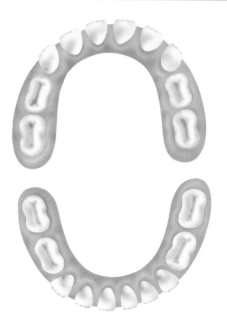

Index